Raene,

May your marriage
be made of all
things beautiful
and blessed!

Carol

THE ABCS OF
LIFE FOR WOMEN

THE **ABCS** OF LIFE FOR *Women*

CAROL WOODIWISS

XULON PRESS

Xulon Press
2301 Lucien Way #415
Maitland, FL 32751
407.339.4217
www.xulonpress.com

Edited by Xulon Press.

Printed in the United States of America.

ISBN-13: 9781545630631

TABLE OF CONTENTS

FOREWORD

It was a typical day. I came home from work and sat down on the couch. I do not nap. I have to be sick or exhausted in order to nap but on this particular day, neither sick nor exhausted, I napped. It wasn't a long nap, maybe ten or fifteen minutes. It was Just enough time for God to tell me what He needed me to hear from Him on that day.

I woke up suddenly and my brain felt like it was in computer mode, downloading information so fast that I jumped up to grab a pad and pen to write it all down. I heard " 'A,' always pray; 'B,' be yourself...." The letters and directions just kept on coming. I struggled to keep up with the information that was flooding my mind. I wrote as fast as I could. There wasn't any time between letters to even decipher what was happening in my mind—and my spirit. I just wrote. By the time I got to "Z," I was exhausted and needed a nap! I took a deep breath and reviewed what God had downloaded through me. It was clear, concise, and seemed important—very important. I wondered what God would tell me next. I waited, I prayed, and nothing. In fact, I waited and prayed for some time after that and still—nothing. Since this was the first time God had ever spoken to me in this manner, I decided to just tuck away my pieces of paper filled with His words and wait. I wish I could tell you that God spoke to me quickly after that day of napping but He didn't. In fact, it was approximately four years later that God would reveal to me what He had in mind.

It was November, 2014. My husband was very ill and I knew it would be soon that God would call him into Heaven. I had been running a business, taking care of my husband, and going to church. I didn't seem to have time for anything else. My flesh was tired but my spirit was strong. I knew that I had to get into a small group at my church and I needed to do it sooner rather than later. Two years before, I had been running my own small groups for nearly two years. I was starving for the rest and refreshment a small group brings. I began to ask my closest friends if they were in a small group. (My world had become pretty small). They were indeed, and I knew of the leader. We had lunch once and I often chatted with her at church between services. I knew she was a woman of God; and I knew immediately that my spirit depended on taking that hour and a half each week for myself. I told my friends, "I will be there." To say that joining that small group was a divine appointment and a spirit-saving move would be an understatement. I was there every week that I could be there. I found rest, love, comfort, understanding, support, and God's presence in one small living room with wonderful women friends.

Jesus called my husband home on April 1, 2015. Thankfully, my small group was there, singing and praying over my husband until my sons and family arrived. I was not alone. God answered my prayer.

Our small group was growing and we needed a bigger living room. My house was perfect—and my friend and I decided to co-teach. I was thrilled! Another answered prayer.

God was beginning to restore my life. There were things I had put on hold while tending to what God had asked of me. He is a faithful God. One study lead to another study; we let the Holy Spirit lead. I have always had a heart for young women who wanted or needed some gentle guidance or mentoring. I mentioned to my friend the words God had given me four years prior, and it suddenly hit me like a ton of bricks (or was it God Himself trying to reach me?) A small group for women—and God—had already given me the title. *The ABCs of Life for Women.* We were due to begin in September. That was our plan. God had a different plan. Our pastor had decided that he wanted our church to participate in an all-church small group on worship. Wonderful! I love worship; but what about my women's group, Lord? I thought we were doing that. I have half of the book written and ready to go. "Wait, really?" OK, I have waited four years; I can wait for a couple more months.

When God moves, He sometimes moves quickly. The next thing I knew, I was deleting all Candy Crush and Jewel Saga from my phone and Kindle, went out and bought a laptop and here I am—writing a book on the ABCs of Life for Women. I don't know at this writing where this journey will lead me, nor am I concerned about it. Whether this book gets published or I am released to lead a women's group now or in the future, I know this to be true: I am being obedient to our Kin and Savior, and I will grow closer to Him and learn more of His word than I know now! Our God is faithful!

Ladies, if you are reading this book, using it for your own small group, or sharing it with a friend, there is one thing I ask you to remember. God can and will use any of us for His purposes. He needs only one thing from us—*we must be willing and available!*

May God bless you with His words. Enjoy the journey. The journey is the only way into His Kingdom and presence. *How will you navigate your journey?*

CHAPTER 1

A

ALWAYS PRAY

I always pray; I don't faint, quit, or give up.
—Luke 18:1

P astor T.D. Jakes is a pastor at The Potter's House in Dallas Texas. He says, "Nothing will teach you how to pray like trouble. Life will make you a prayer warrior."

Have you heard the expression, "Prayer changes things?" I have that saying on a plaque hanging in my house. My life is a testimony of the power of prayer. Prayer has changed my life and my circumstances, and it will change yours. Here's the beauty of prayer. Once you turn your situation over to your Heavenly Father, He can then turn over to you what He has for you. Let me give you an example. Let's suppose you have a birthday gift for someone you love. When the day comes to give that person your gift, you find that they are in a bad mood. You give them the gift anyway and when they open it, there is no joy or excitement on their face. You would feel pretty bad, wouldn't you? When you are holding on to something that isn't good for you and your Father

1

gives you His gift of grace, you have a choice to receive His gift or reject it. Prayer is the tool that will teach you and help you to turn your circumstances over to God so that He can work new things in your life. It is pretty hard to receive new things from your Father if you are still holding on to the old painful ones.

There is a system to prayer. Prayer is not just for telling God all of your woes. Prayer is designed to praise and worship the One who gave life more abundantly. It is important to praise and worship Him in *all* of your circumstances, just as Paul did. Paul tells us that "he learned to be content in all circumstances," whether in chains in prison or preaching the gospel as he was sent to do. It is important to thank God for all He has done for you and for who He is. After all, He is the Almighty One who died to set us free and forgive us from our sins. He died so that we may be free. Prayer is a perfect time to let Him know how much He means to us. God already knows our needs. Our lives, our joys, our pain, our sorrows are not a mystery to our Heavenly Father. He knows every hair on our head. He wants us to come and lay our problems down at the cross; that is when He does His best work. When we release, He goes into action. It is at this point that we must focus not on what is *wrong* but what is *right* in our lives. We are always going to have something go wrong. We live in this world; things go backward and upside down. However, there will always be something for which we can give thanks to Him. The fact that you woke up this morning, the air you breathe, your family, friends, job, church, and nature to name a few.

When I was learning to pray, it was difficult for me. I wanted to sound spiritual. I wanted to sound like some of my prayer-warrior friends. I really struggled. I wanted to be like my spiritual mentor and friend. I prayed for nearly three years for God to make me like her. One day, while I was asking for the one-thousandth time, I clearly heard in my spirit, "I didn't make you like her, I made you, Carol." What a revelation. You mean I can just be me and it's OK? My prayer life soared after that. I realized that God was not going to hear me like anyone else but me. He loves me that much! So now, when I pray, praise, give thanks, seek, worship, and request He hears ME. Thank you, Jesus.

Joyce Meyer, television and conference Christian teacher and motivational speaker says, "We are all waiting for something. God watches *how* we wait." I never forgot that. We humans want everything *now*. We must have faith that God is working in the spiritual realm for us while we are living life, focusing on Him, serving Him, and waiting on His perfect timing and the correct answers for our lives.

We might think we know what is best for us but ultimately God is the only one who knows that. Trust in Him. "Pray without ceasing" does not mean pray all day. It means pray no matter what is going on in your life. Talk to God during the day. Trust Him with your innermost desires and struggles. Thank Him, praise Him, and worship Him. Our God is faithful.

SCRIPTURE VERSES:

Psalm 34:4, 15; Psalm 145:18–19; Isaiah 55:6; Matthew 7:7–8; 1 Thessalonians 5:17; Hebrews 4:16

MEDITATION QUESTIONS:

1. Do you pray? Why or why not?
2. What do you find yourself praying about?
3. Do you balance your prayer life with praise and worship?
4. Do you believe God answers prayer?

3

CHAPTER 2

B

~

BE YOURSELF

So be content with who you are, and don't put on airs.
God's strong hand is on you; He'll promote you at the right
time. Live carefree before God;
He is most careful with you.
—1 Peter 5:6–7 MSG

God made each one of us unique. When we pretend to be like someone else, it is a slap in His face. It is saying to your Creator, "I don't approve of how you made me, what I look like, or how I act." You were uniquely designed for a purpose. Along these lines, Theodore Roosevelt said, "forms of success and achievement lose their importance by comparison." (Nathan Miller, page337, Theodore Roosevelt)

Jesus chose twelve disciples. Each one of them was unique and different. Each one had special qualities and characteristics. Some are well known in the Bible and in history; others are not as well known or written about. All of them, however, made an enormous impact on the kingdom of God during their time.

Peter was the leader of the twelve—he was a Galilean. He is described as "more anxious for honor than for gain, quick-tempered, impulsive, emotional, easily aroused by an appeal to adventure, loyal to the end. Peter was a typical Galilean."

Andrew was second in line. Andrew was the brother of Peter. He was a fisherman before he began to follow Jesus. "Andrew introduced others to Jesus. Although circumstances placed him in a position where it would have been easy for him to become jealous and resentful, he was optimistic and well content in second place. His main purpose in life was to bring others to the Master."

Bartholomew—"The New Testament gives us very little information about him. Tradition indicates he was a great searcher of the Scripture and a scholar in the law and the prophets."

James the Elder—"He was a man of courage and forgive-ness- a man without jealousy, living in the shadow of John, a man of extraordinary faith."

James the Lesser—a little-known disciple. He may have been the brother of Matthew. "James was a man of strong character and one of the fieriest type."

John—"He was a man of action: he was very ambitious, and a man with an explosive temper, and an intolerant heart."

Judas—"It is said that Judas was a violent Jewish Nationalist who had followed Jesus in hope that through Him, his nationalistic flame and dreams might be realized. Judas was a covetous man; at times he used his position as treasurer of the band to pilfer from the common purse."

Jude—"the man with three names." "By character he was an intense and violent Nationalist with the dream of world power and domination by the Chosen People."

Matthew—a tax collector. Little else is known about him. His name means "a gift of God."

Philip—"A man with a warm heart and a pessimistic head. He was one who would very much like to do something for others, but who did not see how it could be done. Yet, this simple Galilean gave all he had."

Simon the Zealot—"Simon was a fanatical Nationalist, a man devoted to the Law, a man with bitter hatred for anyone who dared to compromise with Rome."

Thomas—"Thomas became certain by doubting. By nature, he was a pessimist. He was a bewildered man. Yet, he was a man of courage. He was a man who could not believe until he had seen. He was a man of devotion and of faith." (Bibleinfo.com)

Twelve different men from twelve different backgrounds but they all had three very important things in common.

1. They were not envious or jealous.
2. They were not concerned with rank or what others thought of them.
3. They *all* lived and died for their Master and Savior.

Can we all say the same for ourselves?

Are we more concerned with how our friends, co-workers, and others in the world see us or does it matter more how Jesus sees us? In the end, who will we face, people of this earth or God Almighty? When He asks us who we lived to please, what will our response be?

Ladies, be yourselves! You are beautifully and wonderfully made and you were made *exactly* the way you are for a reason and a purpose. Embrace everything about yourself—your looks, your personality, your gifts, your talents. Everything about you comes from your Heavenly Father. Give Him the honor and glory He deserves by being who He made you to be. If you are curious as to how Jesus sees you, Oswald Chambers says in his daily devotional, *My Utmost for His Highest*, "Notice the kind of people that God brings around you, and you will be humiliated once you realize that this is actually His way of revealing to you the kind of person you have been to Him. Now He says that we should exhibit to those around us what He has exhibited to us."

SCRIPTURE VERSES:

Romans 12:2; 1 Peter 4:4; Galatians 1:10; 1 Corinthians 11:1; Jeremiah 29:11; Psalm 138:8; Psalm 39:14

MEDITATION QUESTIONS:

1. How did God make you? What does the enemy say to lie to you?
2. How do you feel about yourself?
3. What steps can you take right now to believe you are who God made you to be?

CHAPTER 3

C

COUNT YOUR BLESSINGS

I shall find favor, good understanding and high esteem in the sight of God and man.
—*Proverbs 3:4*

There is no better way to begin this chapter than to quote Matthew 5:3–12 from The Message Bible.

> You're blessed when you're at the end of your rope. With less of you there is more of God and his rule.
> You're blessed when you feel you've lost what is most dear to you. Only then can you be embraced by the One most dear to you.
> You're blessed when you're content with just who you are—no more, no less. That's the moment you find yourselves proud owners of everything that can't be bought.

You're blessed when you've worked up a good appetite for God. He's food and drink in the best meal you'll ever eat.

You're blessed when you care. At the moment of being "care-full," you find yourselves cared for.

You're blessed when you get your inside world—your mind and heart put right. Then you can see God in the outside world.

You're blessed when you can show people how to cooperate instead of compete or fight. That's when you discover who you really are, and your place in God's family.

You're blessed when your commitment to God provokes persecution. The persecution drives you even deeper into God's kingdom. Not only that—count yourselves blessed every time people put you down or throw you out or speak lies about you to discredit me. What it means is that the truth is too close for comfort and they are uncomfortable. You can be glad when that happens—give a cheer, even!—for though they don't like it, I do! And all heaven applauds. And know that you are in good company. My prophets and witnesses have always gotten into this kind of trouble.

I believe that the message Jesus is giving us is that we are blessed not by what we have but by the rich inheritance of being his children. The word *blessing* means "God's favor and protection."

The word *favor* means "feel or show approval or preference for." The word *protection* means "A person or thing that prevents someone or something from suffering harm or injury."

We live in a fallen world and sometimes bad things happen to good people. Remember though, our God makes beauty from ashes *all* the time.

Recently, I had a mishap where I broke a bone in my foot and sustained a very bad ankle sprain. I was fortunate enough to not have a cast—only a boot for three weeks. It seemed to take forever for that foot to heal. Most of the time, I am on the go, always doing. A friend suggested that I needed to slow down and maybe that was why I had broken my foot. I began to seek God and ask Him if that was true for me. He had made me like this—I felt happy and productive—so why then did I need to slow down?

In answer to my prayer, the Lord showed me that He didn't care how much I did or how fast I did it—He asked that I not put Him last. I did some repenting that day. There was even a blessing in a broken foot!

There is an old adage that one "can look at a cup as half empty or half full." I suppose that one can also see the good in situations and circumstances or see only the inconvenience of them. I was certainly inconvenienced with a broken foot for nearly a month, but I learned a very valuable lesson. For me, that was a *huge* blessing.

It is up to you to decide how you will look at your life—it's ups, downs, trials and tribulations. The Bible says in John 16:13 "in this world, you will have trouble." Will your *trouble* make you bitter and angry, or will you let God use those troubles for His glory? Lay them down at the cross. Everything was made right by Jesus on the cross. On your best day and on your worst day, count your blessings. Look *up* to the One who loves you and wants to bless you in every way on every day.

SCRIPTURE VERSES:

Job 10:12; Psalm 5:12; Psalm 30:7; Psalm 89:17; Proverbs 3:4; 2 Corinthians 12:9; Ephesians 2:4–7; Hebrews 4:16

MEDITATION QUESTIONS:

1. What is a blessing to you?
2. How are you blessed?
3. When is it hard for you not to see the blessings of God?
4. How can you stretch your blessing "muscle?"

CHAPTER 4

D

DEVOTE YOURSELF TO SOMETHING BIGGER THAN YOURSELF

This is how we've come to understand and experience
love: Christ sacrificed his life for us. This is why we ought
to live sacrificially for our fellow believers, and not just
be out for ourselves. If you see some brother or sister in
need and have the means to do something about it but
turn a cold shoulder and do nothing, what happens to
God's love? It disappears. And you made it disappear.
—1 John 3:16–17 MSG

What drives you? What permeates your daily thoughts?
Do you find yourself going through life on autopilot?
How many seeds did you sow this week? How many people
did you serve? Life is busy! Most of us have families, jobs,
schooling, meetings, schedules and other important com-
mitments which require our attention. There is no escaping
the busyness of life.

Jesus promised us "life more abundant." But Jesus did not mean abundantly busy. "Life more abundant" means His purpose and plans for our lives. Yes, we are given many responsibilities but our first responsibility is to God and our fellow man. We are not here to serve ourselves. We are here to serve each other. When our eyes are fixed on Jesus, we cannot help but serve others. What does serving others look like?

Well, very different than you might think and much easier than you expected. Think of the places you probably frequent each day and throughout the week. The grocery store, Starbucks, restaurants, banks, gas stations, your place of employment, your school, church, retail stores to name a few. With Jesus at the center of it all, we may notice the endless opportunities we have to serve others. A smile, a compliment, a good attitude, a helping hand, paying for someone's coffee, lunch, snack, dinner, or gas—are all ways to serve others. How many carts need to be returned to their rightful homes? How many senior citizens or handicapped people may require a hand? Do you have the gift of baking, cooking, or sewing? Are you handy with tools, gardening, painting, or fixing a car?

I don't remember where I heard the phrase, "What you see, you are responsible for," but I know I use it frequently in my place of business. If we are to live like Christ and have His light shine through us, then we must be responsible for what needs we see around us! Taking time out of our busy day to lend a hand *is* devoting ourselves to something bigger than ourselves. We are being Christ's hands and feet. How do we make this happen? We must fix our eyes on Jesus Christ, take the focus off of ourselves, and take care of our fellow man. The blessings your Heavenly Father will pour out on you when you live a life for others will far exceed your expectations.

Let's take this a step further. Do you attend church regularly? Are you taking up a seat and getting spiritually fat *or* are you using the gifts God equipped you with to serve others? Are you attending, hosting, or leading a small group? My pastor once said, "If you need a casserole, don't expect me to bake you one but someone in your small group will!" Get connected. Serve. Reach out. Be God's hands and feet.

First Timothy 5:6 (ESV) says, "but she who is self-indulgent is dead even while she lives."

SCRIPTURE VERSES:

Genesis 12:2; Proverbs 28:27; Mark 8:34; Romans 12:10; Romans 15:2; 1 Corinthians 10:24

MEDITATION QUESTIONS

1. What have you devoted yourself to? Has it been a benefit to you or others?
2. What can you devote yourself to in the future?
3. How can you make a difference in other's lives?

CHAPTER 5

E

ENJOY OTHERS

When I walk in love God is present.
—1 John 4:12

I think it is safe to say that we absolutely cannot get along with everyone we meet. But it is a commandment from God that we LOVE our fellow man. John 13:34 says, "God has given me one new commandment that I should love others just as He loved me." One cannot argue with the word of the Lord!

In order to enjoy others, we must be in agreement with each other. When even one person in a group is not in agreement, dissension begins and joy leaves. Relationships should be joyful and in balance. Trials will come but when we are in agreement these same trials become opportunities to grow and learn with and from each other. When we are not in agreement, we cannot go through trials and come out joyfully victorious on the other end. Surround yourself with people who are in positive agreement with you and enjoy them.

What about the people with whom we are not in agreement? How do we love them outside of a relationship with them? I think the answer to that question lies in how Jesus loved the Pharisees. He didn't share their table or hand out to them, but He lived in communion with them. He was God in the flesh. The Pharisees were skeptical and religious, everything He wasn't. Jesus, though, did not treat them any differently than His twelve disciples or any of His followers. Jesus held them accountable when necessary, taught them, and loved on them no matter what their agenda was. Jesus didn't have anything to prove. We are going to find ourselves among people with whom we are not in agreement and who may not agree with us. We are to follow the example of Jesus—*love them*. No one is better than another; God loves the humble but hates the proud.

SCRIPTURE VERSES:

Ephesians 4:1–2; Colossians 3:12–14; 1 John 4:7–8

MEDITATION QUESTIONS:

1. Who are some people in your life that you are NOT in agreement with?
2. If you are in a relationship with this person/s, why do you hold on to this person?
3. Is it possible to get into agreement with this person/s? Why? Why not?
4. Who brings joy and agreement into your life? Why?

CHAPTER 6

F

FORGIVE

I condemn not and I shall not be condemned.
I forgive and I will be forgiven.
—Luke 6:37

*F*orgiveness. Big word. *Forgiveness.* Hard to do. *Forgiveness.* Why should I? *Forgiveness.* They don't deserve to be forgiven! *Forgiveness.* Not after what they did to me! These statements sound all too familiar to me. It takes some living to realize that everyone has been hurt in some way in their lifetime. I haven't met one person, not one person who has not been hurt. That is a sad truth. I have been hurt, deeply hurt in my life on more than one occasion. I am not going to say that I was quick to forgive because I wasn't. I voiced each of those above statements at some point in my life. I knew what the Bible said about forgiveness; I read books on forgiveness; I heard sermons on forgiveness, just like I am sure you have. I couldn't understand why I had to be the one to forgive the person who had hurt me. Every time I saw that person or was reminded of the hurt, the same negative, horrible, angry feelings would surface. I would camp out there for a little longer, just letting it all eat away at my heart and my soul.

Then one day, as God would have it, someone asked me if I had read the book *The Shack*. I hadn't even heard of it. The book was a best seller, everyone was talking about it, so I bought it and I read it. I sat down in a chair at 1:00 P.M., opened the book and began reading. I finished the book at 2 A.M.. I couldn't put it down. I read it three times since then. The next three times though, I took my time and let it sink into my spirit. I highly recommend it if you haven't read it. The book is filled with so much wisdom and knowledge but below are two main ideas I would like to highlight:

1. I can forgive and have a relationship.
2. I can forgive and choose not to have a relationship.

Now, number two was a new one for me! No one had ever told me that before. I always thought that if I forgave, it somehow made that person right, *or* I had to subject myself to their actions again and again. Sound familiar? Well, nothing could be further from the truth. Forgiveness is *not* about the person who hurt you. Forgiveness is all about you and your freedom. Forgiveness is key to a life of freedom. Forgiveness sets you free from the snare of the enemy and his control over your life. Unforgiveness holds you a prisoner in your own heart! Once I learned that I could forgive and not be in a relationship, I became free to forgive everyone who had ever hurt me. Some of those people, I chose to confront. I worked through the pain, and learned how to have a healthy relationship with them. The knowledge I gained about what forgiveness really was gave me the control over the relationship and what I wanted to do. That took the power away from the person who had hurt me. How absolutely freeing. I remember a sermon my pastor once gave. He asked us if we had some unanswered prayer in our lives. I was sure we all did, but he challenged us and asked if we also had unforgiveness in forgiven. I made it a point, after reading *The Shack,* to forgive that person without relationship. I gave it up to God. Today, I am happy to tell you that I love this person and we have a good relationship. God is faithful.

The act of forgiveness is power given to you. And lastly, remember, we were forgiven by God Himself. Jesus died that we might live. He forgave us and we must do the same.

SCRIPTURE VERSES:

Colossians 3:13; Ephesians 4:32; Mark 11:25–26

MEDITATION QUESTIONS:

1. Are you holding onto unforgiveness?
2. How do you feel about this?
3. How would you like to feel?
4. Write down everything you feel about this person or situation.
5. Hold this list to your heart. It is your choice. Do you choose to hold on to it or let it go?

CHAPTER 7

G

GET HEALTHY

I will live a balanced life because God's Word state that
if we are not well balanced we open a door for Satan to
come in and devour us.
—1 Peter 5:8

Our mind is our battlefield. Joyce Meyers wrote a book entitled *The Battlefield of the Mind.* It is probably the single most important book a Christian could ever read. All of our thoughts shape us, negatively or positively. We actually become our thoughts. That is a scary reality.

You *do not* have to express every thought that comes into your mind. That's why God gave us a mind, to use it—not to be controlled by it. You actually have control over what you think about and how long you choose to think about it. You absolutely have the power to refuse to think certain negative thoughts. You have the ability to focus on good and positive thoughts. I will admit that this takes some training but it can be done. Make a decision to mediate on things that are pure, noble, and good. Make a decision to cast out any thought that is not healthy for meditation. This is a ploy of the enemy and he will use it every chance he gets if we let him. Satan has already been defeated. Do not give him any power over your mind. He has not earned it nor does he deserve it.

The second area on which you must concentrate is your body. In this fast food, instant gratification society we live in that is one tough feat but if your mind is trained, your body will follow. Your body is a temple of the Holy Spirit and it is your responsibility to keep it healthy. This does not mean that we are out to achieve a size two figure. It means that no matter what our body shape, it is healthy. God created us in all different shapes and sizes; are certainly no surprise to Him. Ask yourself, are you honoring Him in how you take care of what He gave you? Eating the right foods, getting some exercise every day, getting the right amount of sleep, not over indulging, and getting regular checkups are all ways to help maintain a healthy body.

The last area you must concentrate on is your spirit. Remember, what your mind thinks so your body and your spirit will follow. If you love Jesus, you will want to please Him. You will want to get to know Him and spend time with Him. The more you love Jesus, the healthier your Spirit will become. Once your Spirit is healthy and in line with the word of God, the freer you become, the happier you will be! Ladies, once you get a taste of God's freedom in your life, nothing will ever be the same for you. You will never want to be in bondage again! I will leave you with one last thought. This might be a good one to write down and tape to your mirror.

"If it is important to you, you will find a way. If not, you *will* find an excuse." (Quote Archive-Tiny Buddha)

SCRIPTURE VERSES:

3 John 2; 1Thessalonians 5:23; 1 Corinthians 6:19–20; Proverbs 16:24; Proverbs 17:22; Proverbs 4:20–22

MEDITATION QUESTIONS:

1. In order of importance to you, rank the three areas { } body { }mind { }spirit
2. In what areas are you in line with God's word? What areas do you need to improve?
3. What changes are you willing to make?
4. Name one action step you can take to get started in each area.

CHAPTER 8

H

HONOR GOD

*Love the Lord your God with all your heart and with all
your soul and with all your strength.*
—Deuteronomy 6:5

The definition of the word *honor* is high respect, esteem.
Think of the people in your life that mean the most to
you: Family members, friends, co-workers, leaders in your
community, the world, your church, mentors, teachers—
the list goes on and on. We are commanded in the Bible to
"love the Lord your God with all your heart and with all your
soul and with all your strength." As much as we may admire
another person, no one should be above your God. Nothing
should be above your God.

If any person, place, or thing should take the place of
God, you have put an idol in your life. This could happen
without even realizing what is taking place. It can happen
in your thought life, your social life, your relationships,
your job, or any area of your life! In order to honor God, He
must be first in your life. How can we make sure that we

are putting God first in our lives, and what can we do to ensure that we are doing just that? Remember my broken foot story? Well, I got my priorities very straight after that mishap. Below are a few suggestions of how I restructured my prayer life until it became a habit for me to honor God from morning until night.

1. Make sure that when your feet hit the floor in the morning, you thank God for the day.
2. Tape some of your favorite scriptures where you will see them and read them daily.
3. Listen to Christian music while you are getting ready for the day. Worship Him!
4. Pray over all of your meals.
5. Don't stress or worry, pray.
6. Listen to Christian programming in your car. My car is my "war room."
7. Let people know how God is working in your life. This is the best evangelism ever.
8. Thank Him throughout the day and bring Him your burdens.
9. Treat all people with kindness and respect. Jesus did.
10. Ask God to show you His agenda for your day. You will be surprised.

These are just a few ideas of how to get started. Once they become a habit, God will begin to show you many other ways to spend time with Him even while you are having a busy or hectic day. Once God is first in your life and you begin to honor Him, you will begin to notice a change in your life.

You will begin to feel different. Your "highs" will be higher and your "lows" won't be so low. There will be hope and joy replacing discouragement and frustration. There will be peace to replace chaos.

Take an inventory right now of your focus: Worry? Money? Job? Relationships? Family? How much time per day do you think you spend here? What has it changed? The answer is probably, "Not much or maybe nothing at all." God can and will "make all things new." He needs your cooperation! God is a gentleman! He will never force you or coerce you! Open your heart to Him, honor Him every day in thought, word, and action and He will in turn "do a new thing" in your life.

SCRIPTURE VERSES:

Matthew 22:37; Mark 12:30; Luke 10:27; Deuteronomy 30:6

MEDITATION QUESTIONS:

1. Who or what have you been honoring before God? Repent right now and ask God to begin a new thing in your life.
2. Choose at least four of the ten examples listed in this chapter and begin to implement them in your life.
3. Write down the changes you will begin to see in your life, no matter how big or small. Thank God every day when you wake up and every night as you go to bed.

CHAPTER 9

I

INVEST IN YOUR FUTURE

Go to the ant, O Sluggard; consider her ways and be wise.
Without having any chief, officer, or ruler, she prepares
her bread in summer and gathers her food in harvest.
—Proverbs 6:6–8

This is definitely the "reap what you sow" principle. Any area of your life in which you personally invest, using wisdom and discernment, would be crucial to examine. So, let's examine some major areas.

Spiritually: When my boys were young adults, I had a saying written down on a whiteboard in our home, "If you don't feel close to God, guess who moved?" God calls us unto Him but it is our spiritual responsibility to keep that relationship ongoing with Him. We have discussed the ways in which to do just that in the previous chapter. There is an abundance of learning about the ways of the Lord. We can never stop seeking Him and learning of His ways and what He has for us in this lifetime. God is constant and never changing. If we get stuck, it is most likely because we quit growing in His word.

The enemy is always on the lookout to railroad us away from God, His church, and His people. If you want what God has for you, then you must seek Him, praise Him, continue to learn more and more of His word, and put what He teaches you into practice. Invest constantly in your spiritual life. Remember, "Lay up for yourselves treasures in heaven, where neither moth nor rust does corrupt, and where thieves do not break in and steal." (ESV)

Morally: First Thessalonians 4:3 says, "It is God's will that you should be sanctified, that you should avoid sexual immorality. "(NIV) It is an absolute lie of the enemy that women should be sexually active with men outside of marriage. I know that our culture has given men and women its blessing on doing just that but that is not what God's word says. You can tell yourself all day and all night that it is OK, but it is not. God wants women to be pure until marriage. If you were not grounded in God's word with that command, make sure your children are. God is not a punishing God and He forgives *all* of our sins but I believe we break His heart when we give our bodies over to someone to whom it does not belong. Invest in yourself. Are you a convenience to someone or are you God's gift to your husband? The choice is yours.

Physically: I have sons who take very good care of their bodies. They go to the gym daily, they eat right, and show great pride in their appearance. I, on the other hand, have not done such a great job in this area. My youngest son teased me constantly about my lack of physical enthusiasm. I finally got so tired of his teasing that I joined a gym. I have passed the point of looking twenty-five at sixty-five, but I can tell you that I feel better. I have fewer aches and pains and I am hoping to lose some weight that I really don't need to have. I am investing in myself for my seventies, eighties, and God willing, my nineties. I only wish I had invested in myself earlier.

Financially: This is an area on which I can speak from experience. I want to tell you that my late husband and I planned for our financial security but that was not the case. He knew nothing about financial planning and I knew less than he did. Thank God He gave us the common sense to at least take out a life insurance policy. That was one thing we did right in our early years. We lived paycheck to paycheck; we bought things we couldn't afford; we were in massive debt; we didn't save for our future. We didn't have a financial plan at all! God is so good and very faithful; He has a record of saving us from ourselves. In a very long story made short, God brought a Christian financial planner into my life before it was too late. She counseled me, got me on track, taught me, guided me, and made a plan for me to reverse the damage we had done to ourselves. I always tell her that she saved me from myself. It is not too late to put a financial plan into motion. It is not too late to begin to save for your future, your retirement. This is the right and responsible thing to do! God will bless your wisdom. Finally, no matter what—*tithe*. Aside from the life insurance policy that is the second thing I did right.

Relationally: Many gifted and wise people have written books on this word alone. I will be brief but pointed.

How do you treat the people in your life? Do you respect them? Are you kind? Are you considerate? Do you honor them in thought, word, and deed? Do you put them before yourself? Do you thank God for them every day? Are you available? Do you listen to them? Do you pray for them? If you can examine these questions and feel good about your answers, then you are investing in them. If not, put a plan into action and begin to invest in them. When you invest in anything, you get a return. What kind of return do you want from your relationships? You will get what you give.

SCRIPTURE VERSES:

Proverbs 13:16; Luke 14:28–30; Proverbs 27:23; Matthew 25:14–30; 1Corinthians 16:2

MEDITATION QUESTIONS:

1. In what areas of your life are you investing? Which ones need more attention?
2. Where do you sow? What are you reaping? Where is your lack?
3. Of the areas that need attention, which ones will you begin to focus on and invest in? How?

CHAPTER 10

JEWEL—YOU ARE ONE!

For we are God's handiwork, created in Christ Jesus to do
good works, which God prepared in advance for us to do.
—Ephesians 2:10

While enjoying a lunch date with my daughter-in-law, we both discovered that we had the same "soul wound." A *soul wound* is a deep wound that we have received in our life by a person, event, or other situations that left a negative mark on our mind and soul. I dealt with my wound years before, so it was no accident that God gave me a beautiful daughter-in-law in which to share my experience. I would help her to see the jewel that God created her to be. Believe me, she is!

Every person on earth has something in their heart or soul that has been wounded but God says we are His handiwork; we were created in Christ Jesus to do the good works he prepared in advance for us to do. Well, if that is true and the Bible and God's word is truth, we must know that we are a jewel in His mind's eye. How could the God of all creation create anything but the best of the best? Look at the world around you and His creation. From land to sea, it is beautiful and perfectly made. Everything in creation serves a basic purpose and function. Nothing is here by accident or mistake. Everything is useful and necessary. This same principle applies to *you*. You are not here by accident; you are not a mistake; you are necessary, important, perfect and purposeful. You were brought into this life for a very specific reason and you are needed. Someone needs *you*! A certain situation needs *you*! A specific job is waiting for *you*! Your church needs *you*! A friend or family member, maybe a perfect stranger needs *you*! You were created for God's purpose! Do not let the enemy have a foothold in your life with his lies. His lies are meant to keep you from God's purpose for your life. His lies are meant to keep you from being available and accessible to someone or something waiting for *you*! His lies are designed to keep you from giving or receiving all the love God has for you through

Satan has no power. Jesus died to set us free and forgave mankind for all our sins. It is finished. The only power Satan has is the power you give him to rule your thoughts. Take charge of your mind. The most important thought that you should be thinking on is Ephesians 2:10! You are God's handiwork! Philippians 4:8 says, "Finally brothers and sisters, whatever is true, whatever is noble, whatever is right, whatever is pure, whatever is lovely, whatever is admirable-if anything is excellent or praiseworthy-think about such things." Sounds like a most excellent way to live, doesn't it? You can have this life. Surrender to your heavenly Father. Listen to His still, small voice and know that He sees *you* as one of His most necessary and important jewels, created for a purpose which He designed especially for *you*, long before you were even born.

SCRIPTURE VERSES:

Psalm 131:1–2; Proverbs 29:25; Isaiah 26:3; Phillipians 1:6; Phillipians3:3; Joshua 1:9

MEDIATION QUESTIONS:

1. Name one lie the enemy uses to keep you from fulfilling God's purpose for your life.
2. Which above scripture will you choose to meditate on instead of allowing the lies
   of the enemy into your mind?
3. Write down some qualities God gave you. Begin to thank Him.
4. How will you begin to use your God-given gifts?

CHAPTER 11

K

KEEP YOURSELF MORALLY PURE

Flee from sexual immorality. Every other sin a person
commits is outside the body, but the sexually immoral
person sins against his own body.
—1 Corinthians 6:18

This topic is not one that I would have chosen to talk
about. As we all know, it is a loaded conversation piece
in this world of ours today. I know that sexual immorality
goes back as far as the creation of mankind. Why does it
seem so much more justified today? Is it because we are
desensitized by the media? Is it because we have convinced
ourselves that "it's not so bad; we aren't hurting anyone?"
Could it be that we believe because it is so socially acceptable that it is not a sin anymore? There are a hundred justifications to this act of sexual immorality. Satan makes it
very easy and convenient to believe our own lies, especially
when it feels good. Just as there are a hundred justifications
to believing sex outside of marriage is acceptable, there are

just as many scriptures to remind us that sex outside of marriage is *not* what God had intended for you.

I was praying about how to approach this topic God gave me and I was not feeling peaceful or particularly knowledgeable. I decided to just set it aside for a while, knowing full well that God would give me the right words. I was reading one of my devotionals, *My Utmost for His Highest* by Oswald Chambers, when he said, "What do I count in my life 'as dear to myself'?" He was speaking in reference to what the apostle Paul addressed in Acts 20:24, "None of these things move me, nor do I count my life dear to myself." Chambers ends the devotion with 1 Corinthians 6:19, "you are not your own" You are His! In another devotion, he wrote "Anything that does not strengthen me morally is the enemy of virtue within me. Whether I overcome, thereby producing virtue, depends on the level of moral excellence in my life. But we must fight to be moral. Morality does not happen by accident. Moral virtue is acquired.

There are two questions here that you need to ask yourself:

1. Are you His or are you your own?
2. Are you willing to fight to be moral?

No amount of scriptures or lecturing will change the course of your decision if you are not clear on the answer to these two questions. I will leave you with this for prayer and to ask God, your Father in Heaven to help you come to the answers that will bless your life. Holy Spirit, come and fill us with your wisdom and truth.

I am His.

I will fight to be moral.

SCRIPTURES VERSES:

1 Thessalonians 4:3-5; 2 Timothy 2:22; Matthew 5:8; Hebrews 13:4; 1 John 3:3; 1 Peter 2:11; Romans 13:13-14; 1 Timothy 1:5; 1 Corinthians 6:13; 1 Peter 1:22; Galatians 5:19-21; Ephesians 5:3; Psalm 51:10; Ephesians 4:17-32

MEDITATION QUESTIONS:

1. Ask yourself, "Do you want to gain the world and lose your soul?"
2. Where has the world hardened you?
3. What lies of the enemy have you believed?
4. What can you do to prove him wrong?

CHAPTER 12

L

LOVE YOURSELF AND OTHERS

A new commandment I give to you, that you love one
another as I have loved you, that you also love one
another. By this all will know that you are my disciples,
if you have love for one another.
—John 13:34–35

When my son was about five years old he said, "Mom, do you know who I love the most?" Being a first-time mom, I was very excited to hear him say "you Mom" or even his dad. So I said, "Who do you love the most?" He didn't hesitate or even look up at me and he replied, "Well, I love myself best because if I don't love myself, I can't love anybody else." Wow! Out of the mouths of babes! I have never forgotten that conversation from some twenty-seven years ago.

I bring this conversation up from the past because God commands us to love one another. But we don't! We love the people we want to love—the people in our circle or family who are easy to love. What about the *unlovable* people? Why don't we love them? How can we love them?

Examining my own experiences with people, I have found that most people whom I have found unlovable really do not love themselves. They exhibit emotions of anger, bitterness, and sometimes hatred. I have come to realize that these individuals must have been hurt very deeply somehow, sometime in their lifetime. That pain permeates their hearts and souls. My pastor once said, "What's in you will come out of you." We are commanded to love the unlovable. How on earth can we do that?

First: We receive God's love freely. Yet, we have caused grief to God and His Holy Spirit. Even though we have been unlovable, we are not unlovable to Jesus.

Second: We love ourselves and see ourselves through the eyes of Jesus.

Third: We will begin to see others through the eyes of Jesus and be able to love them because God loved them first.

Jesus loves ALL of mankind. He died for ALL of mankind. He did not die for the holy, righteous, pure, good people. He died for ALL. Why? Because like it or not, we are ALL sinners. Our sins may look different from another person's sins. Sin is sin; there is no sin greater than another. Our Savior is greater than our sins. He took it on the cross and He freed ALL mankind. It is finished. Praise Jesus!

Ephesians 5:1–2 (MSG) instructs us on how we should love.

> Watch what God does, and then you do it, like children who learn proper behavior from their parents. Mostly what God does is love you. Keep company with Him and learn

a life of love. Observe how Christ loved us.
His love was not cautious but extravagant. He
didn't love in order to get something from us
but to give everything of himself to us. Love
like that!

SCRIPTURE VERSES:

1 Corinthians 16:14; 2 Corinthians 5:14–15; Ephesians 5:2;
1 John 4:19; Colossians 3:12–14; 1 John 4:12

MEDITATION QUESTIONS:

1. Do you love yourself? Why? Why not?
2. In Ephesians 5, God describes what His love looks
   like. How is God's definition
   of love different from yours?
3. How can you begin to love yourself and others the
   way God loves?
4. How will loving yourself and others change your life?

CHAPTER 13

M

MARRY THE MAN GOD CHOOSES FOR YOU

So God created man in his own image, in the image of God he created him; male and female he created them. And God blessed them. And God said to them, "Be fruitful and multiply and fill the earth and subdue it and have dominion over the fish of the sea and over the birds of the heavens and over every living thing that moves on the earth.
—Genesis 1:27–28

I have done a lot of praying, waiting and contemplating over this chapter. My dilemma lies in what I thought I wanted to say and what was actually the truth! I wanted to tell you that if you marry the man God chooses for you that your marriage would be pain-free, happy, no problems, no troubles, with a storybook ending. That's what I wanted to say. Then, I began reflecting on my own marriage (and I believe that I married the man God chose for me) and I realized that my own marriage was nothing like that at all.

My husband passed away, much earlier in life than he should have, essentially because he did not take care of the body God gave him. He slowly destroyed his body with alcohol and prescription pills. Our marriage was spiritual warfare from beginning to the end. In the beginning, neither one of us knew how to wage war against the ploys of the enemy. In the middle years, I was too busy raising two children and running a business. In the end, I finally learned how to release my husband to God but by then it was too late for him. It sounds sad and discouraging, doesn't it? I had to share this with you to help you understand that even though I had nothing close to a "storybook marriage," there is no doubt in my mind that he was the man God gave me to share my life.

How did I know he was the man chosen for me by God? I do not regret our thirty-two years together. My husband was not delivered from the powers of addiction but within that struggle, I became the woman I am today. Somehow, I always knew how to separate the man from the addiction. He was a man with a kind heart, an enormous amount of love for me and his two sons (and all of his acquired dogs), a gentle man, a man who loved God. He was a creative man; anything he put in the ground grew into something beautiful or delicious.

I became reliant on God for everything; and with this I became stronger, more confident, diligent, and tenacious in my belief that things would get better (although I didn't know what that would look like). My husband was fighting his demons, and I was free to become the woman God created me to be in the meantime. I didn't recognize this at the time. So much of what I know now, I learned during the year after my husband went to Heaven to be with Jesus. He was finally free! God used those thirty-two years to prepare me for life after my husband's death.

This is important to know ladies. If we go into marriage thinking that everything is going to be wonderful all of the time, we deceive ourselves. Marriage is hard work and that work should last for a long time. Divorce is the easy way out! I am not saying that anyone should enter or stay in a marriage where there is alcohol or drug abuse. I was much too naive to recognize that when I married my husband, but God made a way for us to love each other through the good and the bad times.

There are a few reasons women marry the wrong man:

1. We feel like we need a man.
2. We do not want to be alone.
3. We do not want to wait for the right man.

Romans 8:23–28 (MSG) addresses the need to wait.

> That is why waiting does not diminish us, any more than waiting diminishes a pregnant mother. We are enlarged in the waiting. We, of course, don't see what is enlarging us. But the longer we wait, the larger we become and the more joyful our expectancy.

> Meanwhile, the moment we get tired in the waiting, God's spirit is right alongside helping us along. If we don't know how or what to pray it doesn't matter. He does our praying in and for us, making prayer out of our wordless sighs, our aching groans. He knows us far better than we know ourselves, knows our pregnant condition, and keeps us present before God. That's why we can be so sure that every detail in our lives of love for God is worked into something good.

If you do not want to be alone, or you feel like you need a man to take care of you, I strongly suggest that you consider counseling or a co-dependency/enabling support group.

If you get tired of waiting for God's plan to show you the man for your life, I strongly suggest you memorize the above verse! *Anything* God has for us is a million times better than what we think we need or should have.

There are multiple mistakes women make in choosing for themselves. Women may be focusing on the wrong things, or for the wrong reasons, like money, looks, lust, status, company, fantasy thoughts, motherhood, fear (of what? you name it!), desperation, control, belief that time is running out, lack of patience, lack of wisdom, being manipulated, being lied to, and can end up ignoring the red flags they see. The list goes on. Is it such a wonder that so many marriages end in divorce?

I do not know who is reading this—how old you are, or what your past or current relational circumstances are—but urge you to begin to pray for the man God has for you NOW! Believe me, if God created a husband for you, you will find him or he will find you. God will make sure of that. Wait and trust. Our God will *never* let us down.

SCRIPTURE VERSES:

Genesis 2:21–25; Malachi 2:14–15; 1 Corinthians 7:2; Hebrews 13:4; Ruth 4:13; Esther 2:16–17; Luke 2:4–5; John 2:1–2

MEDITATION QUESTIONS:

1. Will you wait or will you settle?
2. Read over the mistakes women make. Have you fallen into any of those traps in dating or marriage?
3. Do you trust God to bring you your husband?
4. If you are waiting, how are you waiting?
5. What can you do to be a better *you* for your husband while you are waiting?

CHAPTER 14

N

NEVER GIVE UP

So let's not allow ourselves to get fatigued doing good. At
the right time we will harvest a crop
if we don't give up and quit.
—Galatians 6:9

I can't count the number of times in my life when I wanted
to give up. Actually, I am in one right now as I write. I
really need to lose some weight! I know that I will feel better,
hopefully, look better, and have a better quality of life. So, I
joined Jenny Craig. This is *not* my first rodeo. It is my fourth
time in ten years, actually. And, ladies, it is always the same
twenty pounds! Ridiculous, isn't it?

That's just one of my stories. But, I am not giving up! I
have lost weight before and I will lose it again. This time, I
plan to try and keep it off.

How many times have you given up on something? It
could be anything—a goal, a job, a career, a church, a friend,
a family member, a difficult situation, a hobby, or even a
dream. We have all given up on something or someone, but

I know that there are also the same scenarios where we *haven't* given up. Do you remember how you felt when you accomplished that goal or dream? I remember more than a few times when I didn't give up. I also remember how incredibly wonderful and fulfilled I felt.

My youngest son had some very difficult teenage years. To say that it was the hardest and most painful season of my life would be an understatement. I cried out to God many times in those days, but God needed a willing participant on the other end. Unfortunately, He didn't have one, so the season lasted much longer than any of us wanted. I remember saying to my son on many occasions, "This is not who you are. I know who you are and who God created you to be. I will *never* give up on you." It was only through God's grace, mercy, and promises that I was able to do just that. I never gave up praying, encouraging, trusting, and believing in God's promise that He personally made to me. I have only heard His voice once; He said, "Be still and know that I am God." I looked up at the heavens and said, "I am trusting you with my son. I am trusting that you can manage him better than I ever could and that your plans for him will succeed." I stood on that promise for two and a half years. I *never* gave up. Can I brag for a moment and tell you that those days were five years ago and now my son is a firefighter, husband, and father-to-be. He is a man of God, and he is my hero. God promises are true if we *don't give up.* I have many other examples that I could share, but I think you can see my point. We only lose if we quit. I can't imagine what the outcome might have been if I had quit on God or on my son. Quitting is not an option for me anymore. Oh, I may procrastinate, get stubborn, drag my feet, or stay in my head longer than I should, but eventually, I want God to have His way in me, through me, and with me. His ways are the best ways. Our plans are nothing compared to what our God and Savior has ready and waiting for us.

Nothing that is greatness comes easy. We have to fight the good fight. We have to stay focused and determined to win. We have to always be on guard for when the enemy comes to "steal, kill, and destroy." When we give up or give in, *Satan wins.* What a horrible thought. But, when we fight, when we put on our armor and stand, *God wins.* Isn't that awesome?

Matthew 7:13–14 (MSG) says, "The way to life—to God—is vigorous and requires total attention." The definition of vigorous is "strong, healthy and full of energy." Isn't that how we need our spirits to be in order to fight the good fight? I would say yes. If you want to live a life where quitting is not an option; if you want to live a life with God at the steering wheel; if you want a life where hopes, dreams, and miracles happen, *keep your spirit strong.*

Never give up! Arm yourself every day with God's word and His promises. He is faithful—He meets us where we are. He is faithful to promote us at just the right time. He will be faithful to finish the good work that began in us at birth. But we must make the decision to fight, to not quit, to not throw in the towel, to never give up. It's a decision ladies, it is a decision that only you can make.

Your harvest will be great; that is God's promise to you and me.

SCRIPTURE VERSES:

2 Chronicles 15:7; Isaiah 41:10; Jeremiah 29:11; Joshua 1:9; Mark 10:12; Hebrews 12:1–3; Philippians 4:13; Matthew 11:28

MEDITATION QUESTIONS:

1. Take a moment to examine your life. What is the dis-couraging area or areas? Why?
2. What area or areas do you thrive in? Why?
3. What action can you take to change your course of action in your discouraging area/areas?
4. What is the most powerful single thing that causes you to quit or give up? Why?

CHAPTER 15

O

OBEY LAWS

*Give to everyone what you owe them.
If you owe taxes, pay taxes, if
Revenue, then revenue, if respect, then respect,
if honor, then honor.*
—Romans 13:7

The definition of submission is "the action or fact of accepting or yielding to a superior force or to the will or authority of another person." Paul writes a letter to the Romans 8:7 that says, "the mind that is set on the flesh is hostile to God, for it does not submit to God's law: indeed it cannot." If we put the two thoughts together, the definition of submission and what the Bible says about submission, it is pretty clear to me that people, even Christians, may have a hard time obeying laws today. Most people will submit to the laws of paying taxes, debts, and revenues but how many of us ignore the simple laws of the land? We ignore the ones that seem to be the easiest, like traffic laws, road signs, laws of respect and honor, laws of the church. How many of us have ignored a stop sign, ran a red light, passed on a double yellow line, disrespected someone in authority, dishonored our parents or an elder, brought coffee into a church that asked you not to, cut in line in a store, or stole something? Do you litter at a coffee shop or drive the wrong way into a gas station when the arrow clearly points in the other direction because we are in a hurry? These may sound like silly little infractions, and sadly, may have become so common-place in our daily lives that we don't even notice anymore. I ask you, "*What would Jesus do?*"

That sounds so cliché doesn't it? But really, "What would Jesus do?" I doubt that Jesus would ever consider acting out on any of the above scenarios! Jesus lived as a man. He followed the rules of the land; He followed the rules of His parents; His teachers; His temple; and He was God in the flesh. What better example for us to have than our living King as our role model? We humans need to *slow down* and think! Why are we in such a hurry to have our way? And again, I am talking about the simple rules in life. I would not want to be one of those who ignore the laws of our government because I would not want to face God on Judgment Day and have to explain my actions for my rebellion. I wonder if we will be held accountable for the lesser infractions. I certainly hope not.

I am a busy person and I have been guilty of many lesser infractions. I had a driving incident that really changed my rebellious attitude to one of humility and obedience. I won't bore you with the details: let's just say it wasn't my proudest moment even though I was right in my feelings. This made me stop and think—how many times have I pushed the limit, ignored a sign, or took a chance I shouldn't have taken? Far too many. God dealt with me on that particular day and I made a commitment to Him and myself that I would obey *all* laws, not just the ones that were convenient for me; not just the ones for which I had time; not just the ones that I liked or with which I agreed. There are laws for a reason. We need laws for order in our world; we need laws to keep peace; we need laws for our safety and security. Things go awry and become chaotic without laws. I don't like red lights any more than the next car but imagine if we didn't have them. I realized that in order to obey laws, I had to become submissive. In order for to become submissive, I needed the help and guidance of the Holy Spirit to convict me when I was acting in and out of my flesh. It took a while and I am far from perfect but here is how I keep myself in check with all laws—I picture Jesus watching me in that situation. Believe me, with that picture in your mind, you will do your best to obey laws—*all laws.*

I know there are injustices in this world of ours, and I detest injustice, but God is my avenger. He will take care of His people. He will right the wrongs and He will redeem and restore. Whether I agree or disagree, understand or not, I obey the laws of the land—from littering to paying all of my taxes. We are under God's authority and we are under man's because God says so. No questions. I heard a wise saying years ago—I can't remember where or from whom, but it is worth repeating: "It is not what we do when everyone is watching, it's what we do when no one is watching." Remember though, God is always watching. That is more than good enough for me. I do not want to disappoint my Creator. I so desperately want to hear the words, "Well done, good and faithful servant." when I stand before Him on Judgment Day. God knows we are not perfect, He knows what mistakes and sins we will make before we even make them. The very least we can do is ask the Holy Spirit to guide us and direct us in our daily lives to make our lives holy and pleasing to God. Obeying laws is a very good place to begin.

SCRIPTURE VERSES:

Romans 13:1–14; Titus 3:1; Romans 2:13; 1 Peter 2:13–17;
1 John 2:4; Luke 20:25

MEDITATION QUESTIONS:

1. What laws do you find easy to keep? Why?
2. What laws do you find difficult to keep? Why?
3. Choose three laws you will work on this week. Ask
   the Holy Spirit to guide and direct you in these areas.

CHAPTER 16

P

PROTECT YOUR BODY FROM ALL WRONG

Be an example to the believers in word, in conduct, in love,
in spirit, in faith in purity.
—1Timothy 4:12

As I was praying and meditating on this chapter, I found myself thinking about our bodies and how we can best protect them. This evening, I was reading one of my devotionals *Come Away My Beloved* by Frances J. Roberts, and I read 1 Timothy 4:12. The Holy Spirit immediately spoke to me, saying, "It's not just about your flesh, it's everything inside and out."

The Word tells us to be examples in "word, conduct, love, spirit, faith and purity." The picture in my mind is one of the whole body, mind, and spirit. If we are to protect our whole body, then let's start with our words. What kind of words flow from our mouths? Are they words of encouragement or discouragement, peace or discord, love or hate, edification or destruction, positivity or negativity? Do our words build up or tear down? Do we speak words of life or death? We must remember our words affect our bodies.

Scientific studies say that many diseases are caused by negative things in a person's life. Negative thinking or living causes stress, and stress causes many sicknesses. We have the ability, through our words, to speak life or death over ourselves and our situations, and over others and their circumstances.

The choice is ours to make. Through the tongue, our words can bring about our outcomes. Let's think before we speak, think before we judge, think before we confess, and think before we condemn ourselves or others. There is death and life in the power of the tongue.

Are we protecting our bodies when it comes to our conduct? What do you let in through your eyes and your ears? Do you listen to good music by respectable artists? Do you watch R-rated movies with more profanity than you care to hear? Do you conduct yourself in a manner that is pleasing to God?

John Bevere once visited our church and I love what he said to his four teenage sons at dinner in one of his stories. He told his sons that there was nothing they could ever do to make their parents love them less, and there was nothing they could ever do to make them love them more. However, the boys were in charge of how *pleased* their parents would be with them. Isn't that *exactly* how our Father in Heaven feels about us? So, check your conduct, ladies, then ask yourself, "Is this pleasing to my Father?"

Do you love yourself? We discussed this question in Chapter 12. If you have prayed and found the love you have for yourself, then you will be quick to express God's love to others through the Holy Spirit *in you*. Protect your body by pouring out the living waters of God's love. Do not poison it with hateful, judgmental, and negative behavior toward others. You not only hurt them, you hurt yourself even more.

Before I surrendered my life to God, I was an emotional wreck inside. My outside, which displayed *happy*, never matched what was happening to me on the inside. God brought a *very* special person in my life some twenty-three years ago. I had never met anyone who displayed daily so much love, joy, peace, and happiness. I didn't know how she did it, but I knew I had to have it. She mentored me even when she didn't know it. Slowly, I began to realize that her love, joy, peace, and happiness came from God. It took me a long time, but I managed, with her patience and tenacity, to achieve what I saw in her many years ago. Thank you, Jesus! Protect your spirit. Pour the Word of God into yourself every day. Feed your soul. Commit your life to Jesus. He is the God of peace. John 14:27 says, "Peace I leave with you: My peace I now leave and bequeath to you. Do not let your hearts be troubled, neither let them be afraid." What a perfect way to protect your spirit.

How do you protect your faith? I have heard my pastor talk about Christians who have walked away from God. How, I wonder, how do you walk away from God? Where do you go? What do you do? What will happen to your life without the One who fights the hardest for you? Walking away from your faith requires letting the enemy in with his lies and schemes. He will try to confuse you, isolate you and fight for your identity. How do you protect your faith? Stay connected to your church, your small group, and the friends that lift you up and encourage you. Stay planted in the Word, your Christian music, your Christian programming. Keep your eyes on Jesus.

Protect your purity. We talked about your body and sexual conduct in Chapter 11. If you need to go back and read it again, and again, and again, please do so! There is something else you can do to protect your purity. Do not put yourself in a position to be tempted. You know what you need to do to stay pure—it's up to you to do it. Stay connected, stay planted, keep your eyes on Jesus. If you do these three things, your body will be protected inside and out! We only have one body and one life. Let's use them to please our Heavenly Father.

SCRIPTURE VERSES:

Proverbs 25:28; Ecclesiastes 5:2; Ecclesiastes 7:9; 1 Corinthians 6:12; 1 Corinthians 13:4–5; Galatians 5:22–23; Colossians 3: 12–14; 2 Peter 1:5–7

MEDITATION QUESTIONS:

1. What areas of your body need to be protected?
2. What actions steps can you take to begin the process?
3. What may hinder you in your attempts?
4. How will you stand up against the ploys of the enemy?

CHAPTER 17

QUIT MAKING EXCUSES

Don't put it off: do it now! Don't rest until you do it.
—Proverbs 6:4

That day, years ago, when I woke from my nap and God was downloading these ABCs to me, I didn't realize how impactful some of these letters would be for my own life. I also didn't realize that there were so many scriptures in the Bible about making excuses.

In researching this particular letter, "Q," I learned that there are at least twenty-five biblical passages for making excuses (from BibleReasons.com). Wow! Jesus knew that His people were going to be very good at this! BibleReasons. com was very interesting and contains great information about this bad habit we humans have. I encourage you to visit it and do some thorough self-evaluation.

God has a slightly different agenda for me to share with you in this chapter. Let me tell what I have learned about excuses.

1. Excuses are evidence of fear or insecurity. How many times in your life have you made an excuse to not do something because you were afraid or insecure? I don't have enough fingers and toes to count those times in my life! Will I be accepted? Will they like me? What if someone can do it better than me? I am not equipped; I will do it, just later God. That's not my gifting or my calling. Why me Lord? Weren't these the words of Moses to God?

Ask these questions of yourself, not only in the spiritual arena but in the arena of life, because no matter where the excuse, someone or something will not be blessed by you.

2. Excuses are the death of dreams and visions. Every time we make an excuse in any area of our life, we kill a dream or a vision that God has placed in us. This can apply to anything from a cleaner house to a huge Joyce Meyer ministry. Excuses keep us stagnant, comfortable, and unproductive. There isn't any way in God's great creation to live out that dream or vision if we are stagnant, comfortable or unproductive.

Our callings are unique and individual. One person will never look like another or accomplish the same things. God has made us for a definite and unique purpose and our excuses stop His flow. A cleaner house may mean a more peaceful house, a happier husband and children. This, in turn, will affect your marriage, your children's future, and may change generations! A Joyce Meyer ministry has impacted the world. According to her own testimony, no one was more fearful and insecure than Joyce herself. Imagine if she let her excuses keep her down.

A world without Joyce—Jesus would cry.

3. Excuses kill hope and stunt growth. I have to be transparent here and tell you that there were more than a few times when I stopped writing this book.

I had many excuses. No one is going to read it. Who cares anyway? I'm not a writer. How am I going to get this out into the world (I still don't have that answer!). This is crazy! You get the idea.

Then, God speaks to me and my hope rises. I write again, and again, and each time, I am awed by His power. God gives me the ability to do what He has asked me to do. If I am not obedient, hope dies, and I quit learning and growing. If the life of just one woman changes because of this writing, my excuses would be a sin.

4. Excuses are roadblocks to fulfilling our heart's passion. I have always had a passion to help people, serve in some way in this world.

As I grew older, a bit wiser, survived some rough times because of the grace of our Father, my passion for helping young women really began to blossom. At one time, I was mentoring four or five young women. We would meet over the telephone and I would do my best to encourage them, pray for them, give Godly advice and wisdom. I would pray that they would not have to do life the hard way.

Our parents give us what they have. They cannot be expected to give us what they themselves do not possess. My mother gave me what she had but there was so much that wasn't given to her as a child, teenager, and young adult, how could she impart to me what she didn't have? So, like my own mother, I had to figure it out. It wasn't easy.

God showed me how I could impart some help from what I lacked myself. It's interesting because what I had lacked seemed to be what these young ladies needed. God will use anyone, anytime, anywhere. I am living proof. If I had let excuses into my head about how unschooled I was, I could not have made a difference, big or small, in the lives of these women. I would never have pursued one of my heart's desires. Instead, today I would be empty and frustrated because a passion that had been put inside of me by God would never have come to fruition. I would not be sitting here writing these words because one excuse would have led to another, and another, until my heart was hardened to what God purposed me for.

God has put a passion, purpose, and calling into your life. Some of you may know what that is; some of you may not yet. But, trust me, it's there. If you are open, God will show you. No matter what it is—*no matter what it is*—go for it. Do not delay. If it is important to you, *you will* find a way. If not, *you will* find an excuse.

SCRIPTURE VERSES:

Exodus 3:11; Judges 6:15; Proverbs 22:13; Jeremiah 1:6; Luke 14:16–24; Matthew 22:2–3; John 15:22

MEDITATION QUESTIONS:

1. What have you been making excuses about?
2. What is stopping you from taking that first step?
3. What is that first step?
4. How will you go about taking it?

CHAPTER 18

R

RESPECT YOURSELF AND OTHERS

Whoever heeds instruction is on the path to life, but he who rejects reproof leads others astray.
—Proverbs 10:17

I have been a believer all of my life. I was raised in Catholic schools, and though I wasn't taught to have a personal relationship with Jesus, I knew from an early age that I loved Him! I went to church regularly, prayed, went to confession, and tried to be "good." Trying to become "good" became too hard for me when I was young. So, as a young adult, I walked away from religion. I never walked away from Jesus, just the rules and regulations of the religion. I was taught to fear God, taught that I was a sinner, and would never be good enough. I was taught that every day, I committed some kind of sin and was going to Hell. That was a long time ago. I wasn't taught of Christ's redemption for my sins or my soul. I just gave up—but I always loved Jesus.

Because I did not have a moral compass in my life anymore, and because I believed that I was never going to be good enough to go to Heaven, I went sideways in many areas of my life! I lived by my own rules and did what I wanted to do. People attract like people—I attracted many people who lived the way I lived, according to their own rules. We were not respecting ourselves, let alone each other. There wasn't anyone to say what was morally wrong; no one was there to encourage us to ask Jesus what He would do; no one to tell us Jesus loves you and wants the best for you and that Jesus came and died to forgive you.

Nothing was said because I chose to hang around people who thought like I did. I eventually married, and made the decision to lead a better life. It wasn't until I attended a Christian church that I heard the words that I longed to hear. Jesus knows that we are all sinners. He knows that we will sin and He knows what we are going to do before we do it. He came and died to forgive you. You are already forgiven. I was stunned. This was truly the Good News! My life changed that day—I never again felt like I had to be "good" or "perfect." I only knew that I had to live the best life I could live and that I would be covered under the grace and mercy of Jesus. It was completely freeing. Of course, I began to seek people who believed the Good News. I began to surround myself with people who wanted what God wanted for them. People attract like people. I now had people to whom I could be accountable. I had good people who, like me, just wanted to please God.

As the years have gone by, children were raised, marriages happened, grandchildren to love arrived, a business thrived, deaths occurred, sorrow and joy were experienced. God has gifted me with respecting myself and those around me. This was a journey for me and a path well-traveled. My rule of thumb was to treat people the way in which I wanted to be treated. And I don't believe anyone wants to be disrespected. I know I didn't.

In the 1980s, the phrase "What Would Jesus Do" became very popular. It sounded a little hokey at the time, but I chose to live by it to the best of my ability. Christ lives in us—correct? So, if we truly believe that the King of Kings lives inside of us and want to live up to how He lived— what choice do we have but to respect ourselves, and in turn others?

When I was a child, I was taught to respect my elders. It really didn't matter how they treated me, but I was to respect them. I can remember despising this at times but I did it, whether I liked it or not. The same can be said for me today. There are some people that haven't have earned or don't deserve my respect. That's all beside the point. If I respect myself, then I respect them. I give them what is due them. No more, no less. I don't have to like them, have relationship with them, or even like giving the respect I give. But I respect them. I am gracious, kind, and thoughtful because that is what I am asked to do by our Lord Jesus Christ.

Learn to respect yourself in thought, word, and deed. We will never be perfect, but God knows our hearts, and He knows when we are striving to please Him. Ask Him for help in any area of your life where you feel you are disrespecting yourself or others. He will come and He will answer, because we are His children and He wants only the best for us. Don't give up if your situations or circumstances don't change overnight. We are all works in progress. Just know that God will never leave us or forsake us. The Word promises us that.

SCRIPTURE VERSES:

1 Corinthians 6:20; Romans 12:2; 2 Timothy 2:15; Galatians 2:20; Proverbs 17:22; 2 Corinthians 12:10; 1 Corinthians 13:4

MEDITATION QUESTIONS:

1. Do you respect yourself? Why or why not?
2. What does scripture tell you about self-respect?
3. Have you asked God to help you in this area of your life?
4. How do you see yourself, your life, different if you gain self-respect?
5. If you respect yourself, how has this quality blessed others around you?
   Or how would it bless others around you?

CHAPTER 19

S

⌣

SERVE

For even the Son of Man did not come to be served, but to
serve and to give his life as a ransom for many.
—Mark 10:45

"For even the Son of Man did not come to be served,
but to serve." What does it mean to serve? The definition of serve is "to perform duties or services for (another
person or an organization." There was a time in my life when
I desperately wanted to serve in my church. Unfortunately,
the church I had been attending picked and chose who they
wanted, and where they wanted them. I was never chosen
for anything and my heart ached. I was complaining to a
good friend of mine about the situation and she told me
that I was already serving every day at my place of business.
She reminded me that every child, parent, and family that
walked through the doors had been impacted because of
my decision to become a teacher. That made me feel a little
better, but I still wanted to serve in my church. Eventually,

I left that church and started to attend another church. I began to serve and I still serve there today.

Jesus came to serve His people. He did not come to this earth to be served. He was born in a stable surrounded by animals. He lived his life as a man and when His time came to go into the world and carry out His Father's business, it was all about serving. He washed the feet of His disciples. He healed, restored, redeemed, delivered, saved, taught, preached, disciplined, prayed, and ultimately, gave His life for all of us.! Jesus came to serve. And we must live our lives in a servant mode.

My friend was correct when she told me that I was serving every day. However, I had never thought about my position in that way. God gave me the ability to be a teacher, and He opened doors for me to have my own place of business. God gave me the platform to serve. God has given you a platform to serve as well. It is up to you to find it, acknowledge it, and serve in that specific capacity. Whether it is in your job, your neighborhood, your community, your church, your family or even on vacation, you were put here to serve. I think most of us have the crazy notion that if our platform isn't big or noticeable, then it isn't important. Nothing could be further from the truth. We must use the gifts God has given us.

Using our gifts is serving. Can you cook? Are you good in the garden? Are you a handy person or a mechanic? Do you have the gift of mercy? Are you a prayer warrior? Do you love children? Do you love to clean or shop? Every time we serve by using our God-given gifts, we bless Our Heavenly Father and His people.

John Bevere wrote a book entitled *Driven by Eternity*. The premise of the book is that we will be judged by how we used the gifts God gave us. We will be judged by our obedience to His will for our lives, and we will be rewarded for our obedience. My pastor has said many times, "don't just take up a seat." We must learn to give out what we take in. Many Christians attend church, small groups, and prayer meetings and take in all they can. They get "spiritually fat," but they do not give out what they receive. They hoard what they possess and no one around them can be blessed by them. How tragic and sad.

I challenge you to get out of your comfort zone. What has God put on your heart? What makes you happy, sad, angry, or frustrated? Those are the exact areas where you are needed. These are the places of the heart. These are the places where you could make a difference. Pray! Ask God to open doors for you to serve. He will—I promise you, He will. Don't be afraid—God will not ask you to do anything that you are not called to do. He calls and then He equips you to be about His Father's business.

Serving is why we were put on this earth. We are not here to take all we can, have a "me" attitude, get ahead fast, live in our flesh. We are here to give, think of others, live right, and stay connected to our spirit. The closer you become to the Father, the more your spirit leads you where He wants you to go.

There is one scripture that I love, Matthew 23:11, "The greatest among you will be your servant."

SCRIPTURE VERSES

Hebrews 6:10; Galatians 5:13; 1 Peter 1:12; 1 Samuel 12:24; Hebrews 9:14; John 12:26; Joshua 22:5; Romans 12:11

MEDITATION QUESTIONS:

1. Are you aware of your God given gifts?
2. Are you using them?
3. In what capacity?
4. If you are not aware of them, ask a trusted friend what gifts they see in you.
5. How will you use what they have called out in you?

CHAPTER 20

T

TRUST YOURSELF

Trust in the Lord with all your heart and do not
rely on your own understanding.
Think about Him in all your ways and
He will guide you on the right paths.
—Proverbs 3:5-6

Let me remind you that I did not come up with these
ABCs on my own. They were revealed to me by God.
When I came to "T"—Trust Yourself, I knew that this was
something we should never do. We can do nothing apart
from God and I know this. I know that Proverbs 3: 5-6 is
very accurate as I have made many decisions based on my
own understanding and got myself in a lot of trouble and
heartache.

So, I asked God, "What do you mean?" I was getting into
bed the other night and my spirit said, "Carol, you can trust
yourself because you always go to God first." The answer
became clear to me at that moment. I mentioned in my

writings that I have made many mistakes, and I have gotten myself into a lot of unnecessary trouble and messy situations. Thinking back, I realized that 99 percent of those times, I did not seek God first. I wanted to do it *my* way. Our way is never the right way. The right way is God's way. When we are seeking God's way and trust ourselves to hear Him, only then can we trust ourselves to do His will.

Let me tell you a true story that will help you understand what I mean. Twenty-four years ago, my husband and I made a decision to move out of California and back to the Midwest where I grew up. It all made perfect sense. It meant a better income for both of us, a better home, and more family around us. We sold our house, moved into a condo until the boys were out of school, and waited for our big move. In the meantime, I had been subbing at the preschool I now own. I wasn't happy there, but I showed up four days a week and tried to make a difference. The previous owner had gotten into a car accident and couldn't work, which is why I was subbing. One evening, I was dusting shelves and she came by. She asked me if I would consider being the director of her school. Of course, I told her no, because I was moving in June. She walked away, and I continued dusting. She came back through again and asked if I would consider buying it.

I was raised Catholic and I knew all about the Holy Spirit. In my mind's eye, He was just a dove flying around the world. In that moment, all I felt was that dove flying over my head and thinking, "No, I don't want to do this, but I had better do it!"

I went home and discussed the possibility with my husband. He wasn't happy about it, but he said to me, "Carol, this is your dream, to own your own school. If this is what you want, then we will stay here." Let me tell you what God did with that one act of obedience—it was probably my very first act of obedience!

1. I purchased the school with not one penny down.
2. We were able to purchase another home in which to raise our boys.
3. The school was not full but filled within the first two months of my ownership. (We have had a 1–2-year waiting list ever since.)
4. He gave me a teacher (friend and mentor) for 24 years and counting.
5. Shortly after hiring her I learned she had prophesied that I would own the school.

Believe me, I did not trust myself at that time. I knew in my spirit that for the first time in my life something bigger was driving this decision. I knew it was not about me or what I wanted. It was trusting in that Holy Spirit moment, no matter how I imagined him in my mind.

Trusting yourself is only safe if you have a personal relationship with God. You must be bringing your life, your decisions, and your all to Him, first and foremost. Then, you can trust in Him that He will lead you and make your paths straight. Only then can you even begin to trust in yourself, because He is in you.

How do we know when God is leading us? I imagine it is different for all of us, but for me, it is a peace that fills me. That's when I know it is Him in me and not me and my flesh. I have grown enough to know that, until I feel that total peace, I need to wait. Confusion is always the enemy. If that happens, I let the thought, situation, etc. go. I take it to prayer. God will always guide us if we can wait patiently, but we want our answers now. Joyce Meyer says, "God watches how we wait." Ouch! I am trying to get better at that!

God knows that we are not perfect. He knows that we will make mistakes and bad decisions. He asks that we come to Him first. He will honor us because He knows our hearts. That is what Our Lord looks at—our hearts. Did we seek Him first? Does it honor Him and His Word? Is it noble, honest, and true? Trust in God; only then can you trust in yourself because "He who is in you" is greater than what is in the world.

SCRIPTURE VERSES:

Proverbs 28:26; Proverbs 12:15; John 15:5; 2 Corinthians 1:9; Proverbs 3:26; Philippians 4:13; Psalm 28:7; Proverbs 20:24; Proverbs 19:21; Proverbs 16:1

MEDITATION QUESTIONS:

1. In whom do you trust? Yourself? The world? God?
2. What does trusting in yourself look like?
3. What does trusting in God look like?
4. Do you need to make a decision to put your trust in God?
5. How will you wait if He doesn't answer you in your due time?

CHAPTER 21

U

USE YOUR GIFTS

Now there are a variety of gifts, but the same Spirit:
and there are varieties
of service, but the same Lord; and there
are varieties of activities, but it is the
same God who empowers them all in everyone.
—1 Corinthians 12:4–6

One cannot argue with the word! First Corinthians 12:4–6 states that there are a variety of gifts and services. To each of us, one is given. Our gift is given to us by God, and we are empowered by God to use them. When we are walking in our gifting, we are honoring God, and we are fulfilled in and through Him. Our gifts are typically easier to discover than we may think. Our gift is what makes us happy, angry, or motivated. It may be a service or activity which comes so naturally to us that we are not even aware we are using it.

Throughout my life, I never felt that I was being used by God. I would look around and compare myself to others; those others typically had a platform or stage. I didn't have a platform, much less a stage. I felt left out and unnoticed by people in my church and by my leaders. I think I was waiting for someone in leadership to notice me, call me out, and tell me what my gift was and how I could use it. I spent so much time searching, comparing myself to others, and feeling left out and sorry for myself, it is amazing that I can remember now how God was using me the whole time. I didn't realize it then, because using my gift came so easily to me. Here are a couple of ways God used me—despite me.

I had a neighbor who was pregnant and nearly homeless. We took her in and loved and cared for her and her baby. We helped her get a job, her own apartment, and to go back to school.

God gave me my business shortly after that. It was a successful business that He has blessed beyond measure. After twenty-four years, it is still not a job but a service given to me by God. He gave me the heart to serve and love on people, and that is what I did. I mentioned earlier that I love to mentor young women. God brought young women into my life, and through many conversations, I brought wisdom, discernment, and healthy outcomes to their lives. It was God in me, not me, because I was too stuck to even realize He was using me in my giftings. The Bible says in Numbers 22:21-39 that God used a mule to make his point. How true a statement.

Recently, I was at church and my pastor was highlighting eight families in our church and matching them up with our mission statements. By number seven, I was feeling pretty discouraged and condemned. I hadn't done any of those things: missions, working with homeless people, feeding the hungry, etc. Just when I was about to cry in my spirit, the pastor highlighted a dad. This man had come from a hard life with drugs, jail, prison. He found the Lord and turned his life around. He married and had three sons. He raised his sons in the church. He fed them the Word, he encouraged them in the Lord. My pastor concluded this testimony with these words, "This dad left his legacy to his sons." That was the eighth and final highlight. I almost had to leave my seat. The tears came up hard and fast when I realized that was me! I didn't have the hard beginning of this father but I had two sons and I raised them up in the church to the best of my ability. I love my sons with every fiber of my being, and in many ways, I dedicated my life to them and still do as they have now moved into manhood, fatherhood, and their own destinies. I have left my legacy with my sons. I am far from perfect, but my sons know that I love the Lord. I serve Him, trust Him, honor Him, and depend on Him for everything. It isn't hard to find and use your gift. If you are open and available, God will guide and direct you.

Every gift is important to Him—that is why you were created. Please do not wait for a platform or a stage. Please do not wait for someone to notice you or affirm you. Be yourself and do what comes naturally to you. Act on your passions and your abilities. Start somewhere, no matter how small or insignificant it may seem. My first real job at my church was collecting papers and faxing them over to the main office. This led to helping at the Information Counter on Sundays, and that led to being in charge of the Information Counter for six years, God is a faithful God and He will give us the desires of our hearts. He has never let me down and He won't let you down.

I have found over the years that our gifts and abilities never change but where and how they are put to use will change. I have learned that there are seasons of rest and seasons of great abundance. I have learned to trust God in all seasons. God has used me in many ways throughout my life only because I was open and available. He will use you and the gifts and abilities He gave you too. Why else do you think you are here?

SCRIPTURE VERSES:

1 Peter 4:10; Romans 12:6; 1 Timothy 4:14; Matthew 25:14–30; Matthew 5:14–16; Colossians 3:23–25; Proverbs 18:16; 2 Timothy 1:6; Matthew 25:29; Ephesians 4:7

MEDITATION QUESTIONS:

1. What drives you? Motivates you? Makes you happy or angry?
2. Do you know what your gifts are?
3. Are you using your gifts? Why? Why not?
4. What action step will you take to either find your giftings or begin using them?

CHAPTER 22

V

VACATION

By the seventh day God had finished the work he had
been doing: so on the seventh day he rested from all
his work. God blessed the seventh day and made it holy,
because on it He rested from all the work he had done.
—NIV

The Bible doesn't use the word *vacation*, but when we
think of a vacation, rest is usually one of the main ingre-
dients we humans want and need during that time. I think it
is safe to say that if God rested on the seventh day after His
work was done, we are also free to do the same. Jesus rested
also. In Mark 6:31, Jesus says to His disciples, "Come with
me by yourselves to a quiet place and get some rest." Maybe
Jesus didn't need rest, but He certainly knew His disciples
needed it! Not only did Jesus invite them, He gave them the
gift of rest and refreshment.

Have you ever met someone who works all the time?
They are the person you wonder about—do they ever rest,

slow down, or take a break? I've wondered—and not just about one person but quite a few. These people usually lack peace and contentment. They are so busy working, making money, or trying to impress their superiors that they are missing out on other very important aspects of their life. These people are missing out on family, children, friends, church, fun, and most importantly, refreshment. I love anything that speaks of our souls being well. It is well with my soul. When we are rested and refreshed, our souls are also rested and refreshed. We can focus on our Savior and His love and grace. If we are constantly on the move, how are we to know Him, to hear His still, small voice, to worship Him, and spend time in prayer?

When I was raising my sons, we didn't have a lot of money to go on vacations. What we did do was get away as often as possible to rest and refresh ourselves from the daily grind. We would hike, go to the city, museums, camping, dirt bike riding; we took a lot of day trips. I remember a time when my husband wanted to go to the beach and I had my mind set on cleaning the house. I admit that I had a hard time recognizing the need for rest and refreshment in my younger days. I was adamant that we should clean the house and he was adamant that we go to the beach. He finally said, "Then the boys and I will go without you and you can stay home and clean the house." That was fine with me. But, as they were all getting ready to go, their excitement mounting, I began to feel left out. Long story short—we all went to the beach that day. It was a day I am happy to say I didn't miss. The Bible also says in Ecclesiastes 3, "that each of them may eat and drink and find satisfaction in all their toil—this is the gift of God."

Vacationing is a gift from God. Your vacation may look different from someone else's. Ours sure did—we did it the only way we could afford. Looking back on those days, "it was well, with my soul." I felt peace and contentment. I loved spending time with my sons, watching their joy and enthu-siasm with every outing my husband came up with. My sons are grown men with children of their own and that's what they remember most fondly about their dad—the adven-tures and experiences he took them on.

So, take vacation; rest; refresh. God rested, Jesus rested, and we are to rest too. It is a free gift from Heaven—don't miss out. You will be a happy and contented wife, mother, sister, aunt, and friend. Your church will thank you for it and so will the people who love you.

SCRIPTURE VERSES:

Proverbs 3:23–24; Psalm 139:9–10; 2 Corinthians 8:16–19; Psalm 121:7–8

MEDITATION QUESTIONS:

1. What thoughts or opinions do you have about vacationing?
2. Are they in line with the word of God?
3. Do you take time for rest and refreshment? Why? Why not?
4. What benefits would vacationing have for you personally?
5. What kind of vacations are possible for you?

CHAPTER 23

WEATHER YOUR STORMS

It is the Lord who goes before you. He will be with you,
He will not leave you or forsake you.
Do not fear or be dismayed.
—Deuteronomy 31:8

In John 16:33, the Lord says, "I have told you these things, so that in me you may have peace. In this world you will have trouble. But take heart! I have overcome the world."

Don't you sometimes wish that you didn't have to believe *everything* the Bible says? Well, it is the word of God and we either believe all of it or none of it. We certainly cannot pick and choose what we will and will not believe. Therefore, we know that *everyone* has trouble in their life. *Everyone.*

I have shared much of my life with you ladies in these chapters but not all of it. My life has had an abundance of joy, peace, happiness, contentment, grace, favor, and blessings. My life has also had more than it's fair share of pain, heartache, disappointment, worry, fear, and struggles. Through most of it, I didn't know who my God was. When God began to draw me to Him and I began to know Him, I saw His hand in absolutely every aspect of my life. I recognized the times He carried me, graced me, set my feet down, and let me revel in happiness, protected me. He kept His promise to me—He never left me, He has never forsaken me.

My oldest son invited me over for a barbecue; his friends were there and we were having a fun time. My son began to reminisce about his dad and the good times he remembered as a child. My son acknowledged he knew his dad well. He said that he chose to remember the good times. Then, much to my surprise, he told me that what he learned most from me was how I never gave up, how I always stayed true to his dad and the family. He credited me for teaching him how to be a better man. He thanked me for never giving up on his dad and our family, even though he fully realized how difficult that had been. With tears in my eyes, I thanked him. We both knew, however, that there was only *one way* I managed those things—because of the grace of my Father! Even now, I look back on some of the hardships and wonder at how I came through them. Of course, I know, but the wonder is about how good my God had been to me; how carefully he orchestrated every detail, how lovingly he equipped me with the right thing at just the right time. The most precious gift my Father ever gave me was HOPE. I have a plaque in my house that reads, "Never let go of hope. One day you will see that it has all finally come together. What you have always wished for has finally come to be." Thank you, Jesus, for the gift of hope. "Hope deferred makes a heart sick." My heart is happy, content, and full of peace and joy.

We cannot weather our storms if we focus on them. We must keep our eyes on Jesus, the author and finisher of our faith. While we are going about the work of Jesus, He is going about our work. He is working it all out in the heavens. We will have our feelings and emotions and we should. When we camp out in these emotions for long periods of time, it breaks the heart of our Father. He came and died so that we may be free. We are not free if we live in the eye of the storm. There are a few things I try to practice when a storm arises. 1) I remind myself to whom I belong; 2) I worship and praise anyway; 3) I tell myself over and over that God is in control, not me; 4) I pray; 5) I remember the last victories; and 6) to the best of my ability, I surrender it all to Him.

I promise you that these make every storm easier to get through! It's only when we take our eyes off of Jesus and try and take matters into our own hands that the seas become so rough that we feel hopeless. Hopelessness is not what God intended for us. The following scriptures will encourage you. I suggest that you to type them out and tape them up where you can read them every day. Weather your storms with the promises of God.

SCRIPTURE VERSES:

Psalm 107:28–31; Nahum 1:7; Isaiah 25:4–5; Psalm 91:1–5; Exodus 14:14; Psalm 46:10; Joshua 1:9; Deuteronomy 31:8; James 1:2–5; 2 Corinthians 4:8–10

MEDITATION QUESTIONS:

1. What is your current storm?
2. How are you handling it?
3. What do you need to change?
4. What keeps you strong?
5. Do you trust God?

CHAPTER 24

X

———⌣———

EXEMPLIFY INTEGRITY

Let your eyes look straight ahead, fix your gaze directly
before you. Give careful thought to the paths for your feet
and be steadfast in all your ways .Do not turn to
the right or the left, keep your foot from evil.
—Proverbs 4:25–27

The definition of integrity is, "the quality of being honest
and having strong moral principles, moral uprightness."
"The state of being whole and undivided." Synonyms—unity,
unification, coherence, cohesion, togetherness, solidarity.

Integrity has become a very important word in my life.
Why? It's important because for many years, I lived without
it. I thought that because I was basically a good person, I
had integrity. How wrong I was. Being good has nothing to
do with integrity. Integrity is bringing who you are, what
you are, what you believe, how you act, react, and manage
your life to the table every single day to every single person.

That means in order to have integrity, you must first know who you are in Christ. If you do not have that first principle, you will not live a life of integrity. You will most likely be controlled by your feelings, your emotions, and your circumstances. Jesus walked in integrity for his thirty-three years on earth. He was always His Father's Son. He did not change who He was or how He responded or acted, no matter who was in front of him. Whether He was with His disciples, in the temple teaching, with the Pharisees, even as He stood before Pilate to fulfill the Scriptures, Jesus was Jesus. He lived a life of integrity. He was honest and true to Himself (His Father). He had strong moral principles and uprightness. There is nowhere in Scripture that describes Jesus any different than who He was. We are human and we all have sin in our lives because we are not Jesus but does that mean that we can act any way we desire? I think not.

I recently went through a season where I was attacked and deceived by someone I trusted. For four days, I was sick, confused, scared, and upset. I lost track of God and His plan for my life. I was totally reacting out of my flesh. Then, a faithful friend said to me, "You are not going to let this person take away what God has already promised you." That was it. I was back up on my spiritual feet and ready to war, with integrity! I prayed; I sought God's will; I stood firm and took back the ground that was slowly being taken from me by the enemy. I declared, "I am going to be Jesus in this situation."

To the best of my human ability and with God's grace, the whole situation worked out in my favor and God restored. I am far from perfect—far from perfect, but I have come to know that I am a child of God and when He does work in me, I know it. I know it because I know that I couldn't do it! I have a Scripture that I love and it helps me to walk in integrity—every day, in every way, to every person. They get the same me, no curve balls, no surprises, just me with all my flaws and hang-ups. But it's me. The Scripture is Luke 6:31, "Do unto others as you would have them do to you."

I don't want fakes, phonies, liars, cheats, angry, dishonest, or immoral people in my life. Therefore, I won't be one of those people. I don't want mean, hateful, judgmental, critical people in my life. Therefore, I won't be one of those people. We all make mistakes but Jesus came and died for all of our mistakes. But patterns, good and bad, make us who we are. I choose a life of integrity.

Years ago, there was a TV program entitled, *Touched by an Angel*. I loved that program. In one episode, Monica, one of God's earthly angels stood before God after a struggle with an assignment that God had given her. She was torn between her feelings and God's will. She stood before Him, a pathetic mess, and God stood in all of His glory. Monica wept before the Lord. She asked her questions, she asked for forgiveness, and Jesus said to her, "Well done, good and faithful servant."

In that moment, I knew that no matter what, I wanted to hear that from Jesus when I enter the Kingdom. I want to hear those words, "Well done, good and faithful servant." So, I choose to live a life of integrity. God looks at our hearts. He knows our motives and our intentions. He is quick to forgive. He rejoices when we repent.

SCRIPTURE VERSES:

Proverbs 11:3; Proverbs 28:6; 1 Peter 3:16; Proverbs 12:22; Proverbs 21:3; 2 Corinthians 8:21; John 14:6; Hebrews 13:18; Psalm 41:11–12; Philippians 4:8; Isaiah 26:7

MEDITATION QUESTIONS:

1. What does the word *integrity* mean to you?
2. Have you lived a life of integrity?
3. What areas of improvement do you see?

4. Do you think it is important to God to live a life of integrity?
5. Do you "do unto others as you would have them do unto you?"

CHAPTER 25

Y

YIELD YOURSELF TO GOD

Then Jesus said to His disciples,
"If anyone wishes to come after Me,
He must first deny himself
and take up his cross and follow Me."
—Matthew 16:24

B eing raised Catholic, I used to think that if we denied ourselves, it meant that we had to suffer or sacrifice everything we loved or that gave us pleasure. That thinking was what prompted me to walk away from my religion and church for a very long time. I loved God and Jesus, but I was afraid of Them and the power they had to throw me into Hell for any infraction.

It wasn't until I met my husband that God began to reveal to me who He really was. My husband brought me into every church he could find until we found the one that was right for us. I was terrified because I thought that by being in any church but the Catholic Church, should I die that day, I would go straight to Hell. (I really don't know where that belief came from.)

One day, visiting yet another church in our town, the pastor said that God knew we were sinners, and He came to die for our sins (I already knew that). God knew we were not perfect; we would continue to make mistakes and He was ready to forgive us. Halleluiah! Music to my ears! I thought, "now *that* I can do." Little did I know, but it was the first time in my thirty-plus years that I had heard a grace message. I was hooked. It took me a whole lot longer to learn to have a personal relationship with the Father but at least I was on the right track again. Fast forward many years and the learning continued, sometimes slowly, sometimes in waves, but nonetheless, I kept growing and understanding more and more.

Yield is another word for *give*. So, give yourself to God. What does that look like? How do I do that? I like parts of my life. Do I have to give them up? What if He sends me to Africa? What if He asks me to sell my house and all of my possessions? I struggled with some of those questions. When I look back on them, I realize how ridiculous my concerns were. First of all, if He calls you, He equips you! If He calls you to Africa, it's because you have a heart for Africa. If He asks you to sell your house and give up your possessions, it's because you know that there is a yearning in your spirit to rid yourself of those things for a higher calling. God will not call you outside of your heart's desire. You may not be aware that a particular yearning is there until you make that first trip to Africa, but God calls us where we will be fulfilled. We may think that money, location, and possessions are what we want and need but if any of those things get in the way of God's calling in our lives, He can and will make sure there is an opportunity to show you a better way. God will always let you choose for yourself, He will never force you! Let me tell you, His way is the only way to joy, peace, contentment, and fulfillment.

Yielding yourself to God simply means to give Him the decisions of your life. Pray about everything. He is in every detail. I have so many stories of God's direction in my life but I will share just one recent one. I was ready to sell my house and downsize. My sister-in-law was ready to buy my house. What a blessing! Everything was going great and suddenly, *everything* fell apart. I knew then that God had something else in mind so I just yielded and said, "OK, God." Two weeks later, my son phones to tell me that he and his wife are going to look at a house. They had no intention of moving, they were getting ready to add on to their home. The next phone call I get is one of pure joy and excitement! They loved the house, they decided to fix up their house, then buy the new one. One problem—where will they live with their 2-month-old while their house is being fixed up? Guess who had plenty of room because she had not yet downsized? *Me*, of course. My son, daughter-in-law, and new granddaughter lived with me until they were able to move into their new home. In the meantime, I did put an offer in on the same house I had been interested in (yes, it was still available), and my sister-in-law purchased my home. No muss, no fuss, no bother. We moved within two weeks of each other. I wouldn't trade that time I had with my family for anything. It meant the world to me and to them. God gave us the desires of our hearts. We are all happy in our new homes. Mine, "cozy, cute" as my niece dubbed it; and theirs—two-plus acres, complete with three dogs and a hot tub! God is good, all the time!

Trust God's plan for your life. When He closes a door, He really does open a big window. Yield your ways and plans to Him—His are better. His plans are designed for you. Learn to wait. Learn to pray. Learn to listen. You will be blessed beyond measure, or may be protected from something you couldn't foresee. Yield yourself to God. You couldn't be in better or more capable hands than the God of the universe.

SCRIPTURE VERSES:

Psalm 100:3; 1 Chronicles 29:14; Deuteronomy 8:18; 1 Timothy 6:17; Romans 12:1; Proverbs 23:26; Psalm 40:7–8; Luke 14:33; Philippians 3:8

MEDITATION QUESTIONS:

1. Is it frightening for you to yield yourself to God? Why? Why not?
2. What areas of your life would be difficult for you to yield?
3. What areas of your life are you ready to yield?
4. Have you had experience in yielding an area of your life? What did that look or feel like for you?

CHAPTER 26

Z

BE ZEALOUS

Brothers and sisters, my heart's desire and prayer to God for the Israelites is that they may be saved, For I can testify about them that they are zealous for God, but their zeal is not based on knowledge. Since they did not know the righteousness of God and sought to establish their own, they did not submit to God's righteousness. Christ is the culmination of the law so that there may be righteousness for everyone who believes.
—Romans 10:1–4

Z ealous! Fervent, ardent, fanatical, passionate, impassioned, devout, devoted, committed, dedicated, enthusiastic, eager, keen, vigorous, energetic, intense, and fierce. What are you zealous for?

{ }Family

{ }Money

{ }Success { }Job

{ }Spouse { }Boyfriend { }People

{ }Material things

{ }Church

{ }Nature, animals

{ }Food

{ }Entertainment

{ }Travel

{ }God

{ }Approval

{ }Salvation

{ }Promotion

{ }Sports/activities

{ }Spending time with God

{ }Serving

Take an inventory of the above. With "1" as the highest to "10" as the lowest, rank each of the above categories in your life by their importance. Be honest with yourself.

Readers, you have stayed with me for twenty-six chapters. I have given you all that the Holy Spirit has asked me to give. What I have offered to you is a life of freedom and love. Peace and joy. Will it be without trouble? I don't think so. But does it offer hope and salvation? Yes, it most certainly does.

In my foreword, I asked a question. I am going to ask it again. It is the most important decision you will make for your life.

How will you navigate your journey?

The choice is yours. God awaits you. He has great plans for your life. I pray that you will be blessed and anointed by these ABCs of Life. I pray that God will grab you by the strings of your heart and draw you closer than you have ever been to anyone or anything in your life. May the Lord God, your Father, grant you the desires of your heart as you pursue a love relationship with Him.

May He bless and keep you under the shelter of His wings as you walk with Him on this earthly journey. My prayer for each of you is that when you stand before our God on Judgment Day. He will look you in the eye and say, "Well done, good and faithful servant."

APPENDIX

Leader Group Study Questions—Chapter 1

1. What did you learn about yourself and prayer in your discussion?
2. How did the conversations of others affect you?
3. Will this session change your prayer life? How?
4. What will you do differently in your prayer life this week?

Leader Group Study Questions—Chapter 2

1. Name one thing you have learned about yourself in your group. What lie have you been living?
2. Who is the real you that you want people to see?
3. Name one action step you can take to change your old way of thinking and acting.

Leader Group Study Questions—Chapter 3

1. Talk about your last blessing.
2. When was the last time you blessed someone?
3. Have you seen blessings in your trials?
4. How can you practice finding beauty in ashes?

Leader Group Study Questions—Chapter 4

1. Is Jesus the center of your life?
2. Are you using the gifts God equipped you with for others?
3. Name one or two actions steps you will take this week to live for others.

Leader Group Study Questions—Chapter 5

1. Much of life is a series of our own choices. What did you learn about yourself and the people with whom you surround yourself from this chapter?
2. Is there an action step you can take this week to enjoy the people in your life?

Leader Group Study Questions—Chapter 6

1. If you would like to read your list—let's do it! Louder; *louder*!
2. Ask God to help you to forgive and be set free.
3. If need be, take the list home and repeat as often as necessary. When you feel released and free, tear it up and let it go! You are now no longer a prisoner!

Leader Group Study Questions—Chapter 7

1 .Name one area you will take control over this week.
2. Pick someone you know and trust and who will be honest with you to help hold you accountable to your decision.
3. Name one negative thought pattern you have. Write a short prayer you will say when this thought comes into your mind.
4. What new spiritual strategy will you use to help strengthen your spirit this week? (Examples: music, devotionals, Christian programming, reading the Word, praying more)

Leader Group Study Questions—Chapter 8

1. How did you honor God differently last week?
2. Did you notice any changes in yourself because of it?
3. What four strategies did you choose?
4. Which worked the best for you?

Leader Group Study Questions—Chapter 9

1. You have all chosen some areas where there is lacking in your life. What steps will you take to begin reaping in these areas?
2. Do you believe God when He says in Luke 6:38, "I give, and gifts are given to me; good measure, pressed down, shaken together and running over. For with the measure I deal out, it will be measured back to me?" Why? Why not?

Leader Group Study Questions—Chapter 10

1. What scripture did you choose to meditate on?
2. Every day this week, choose one quality or gift that God has given you. Thank Him daily for these gifts. Thank Him that you are His jewel.
3. How do you think God sees you?
4. How do you see yourself?

Leader Group Study Questions—Chapter 11

1. If Jesus were in the room, name one thing you would want to change in your moral life.
2. In some cases, you may have to make the decision to change your circle of friends, some relationships, your entertainment, etc. Are you willing to make these changes? Why or why not?

3.Would you be willing to ask God to send His Holy Spirit into your life to help you correct your moral wrongdoings? Let's do it now!

Leader Group Study Questions—Chapter 12

1. What's in you comes out of you. What came out of you this week?
2. How did you love differently this week?
   Do you feel that you loved yourself and others the way God loves?
4. Was this difficult for you? Why? Why not?

Leader Group Study Questions—Chapter 13

1. Did you reflect on your questions in this chapter?
2. What did you learn about yourself?
3. Is waiting on God difficult for you? Why?
4. Do you trust that God has a plan for you and a husband? Why? Why not?
5. Have you begun to pray for your husband?

Leader Group Study Questions—Chapter 14

1. Think of a time when you wanted to quit but you didn't. What drove you to persevere?
2. What regrets have you had because you quit something that meant a lot to you?
3. Choose an area that you may have given up on but can now go after it. How will you begin your journey of success? Write down what may stop you and begin to pray against those things right now and through your success journey.

Leader Group Study Questions—Chapter 15

1. By obeying simple laws, have you seen any changes in the people around you?
2. How do you feel since you have been guided by the Holy Spirit to obey laws ?
   Do you take Jesus with you in these law-abiding areas? Has He made a difference? How?

Leader Group Study Questions—Chapter 16

1. In the areas you chose to protect, how is your life different now?
2. Are you feeling a correction from the Holy Spirit if you slip? Do you take the correction? Do you fight it?
3. Have you found that protecting your body has changed your circumstances? Your life? In what ways?

Leader Group Study Questions—Chapter 17

1. What action step did you take this week to move to your call?
2. How has the enemy tried to stop you from moving forward?
3. How did you defeat his lies?
4. What one thing do you feel different about since your decision to stop making excuses and start moving forward?

Leader Group Study Questions—Chapter 18

1. What inventory did you take in self-respect?
2. What action step did you decide to take?
3. How did your step affect those around you? Or did it?
4. Is it difficult to respect yourself or those who you feel don't deserve respect?
5. How will you change this in yourself?

Leader Group Study Questions—Chapter 19

1. How have you been using the gifts God gave you?
2. How has using your gifts blessed others?
3. Are you guilty of becoming "spiritually fat?"
4. What will you do to change this pattern in your life?
5. What has stopped you from using your gifts?

Leader Group Study Questions—Chapter 20

1. Where has not trusting in God gotten you?
2. How would your life look different if you began trusting in Him?
3. Why is it difficult for you to put your trust in God?
4. Do you believe that God will "never leave you or forsake you?"

Leader Group Study Questions—Chapter 21

1. Do you find yourself comparing yourself to others?
2. Are you looking for a platform or validation from man?
3. What are the desires of your heart?
4. After reading this chapter, can you see how God is already using you, and your gifts and abilities?
5. How will you advance from this point?

Leader Group Study Questions—Chapter 22

1. What did you learn about vacationing in this chapter?
2. Will it change the way in which you live?
3. How do you see your life changing if you took time to rest and refresh?
4. How will it affect your relationships and your prayer life?

Leader Group Study Questions—Chapter 23

1. How do you think your life would change if you trusted God with your storms?
2. Is this easy for you to do? Or is it difficult? Why?
3. Name some victories God has already brought to you?
4. What are some advantages to weathering your storms?
5. What are some disadvantages to weathering your storms?

Leader Group Study Questions—Chapter 24

1. What attitudes and motives do you need to change in your life?
2. Name one area of your life where you need to practice integrity?
3. What does a life of integrity look like to you?
4. How will your circumstances, situations, or life be changed if you model integrity?

Leader Group Study Questions—Chapter 25

1. What does it mean to you to *yield* yourself to God?
2. Did you find areas this week that you *yielded* to God?
3. Did yielding change anything about your life, thoughts, feelings, actions?
5. Do you feel that you can yield yourself to God when you are operating in your flesh? Give an example.

Leader Group Study Questions—Chapter 26

1. Were you surprised by the ratings you gave each category?
2. What will you change?
3. How will your life look after your changes in priorities?
4. What is your number one priority? Why?
5. What area did you find the least important after careful consideration?

CPSIA information can be obtained
at www.ICGtesting.com
Printed in the USA
FSHW010001010219
55388FS